The sea around me . . .

_____

the hills above

BOOKS BY ROD MCKUEN

POETRY
*And Autumn Came
  Stanyan Street & Other Sorrows
  Listen To The Warm
  Lonesome Cities
*In Someone's Shadow
  Caught In The Quiet
  Fields of Wonder
*And To Each Season
  Come To Me In Silence
  Moment To Moment
*Celebrations of The Heart
*Beyond The Boardwalk
  The Sea Around Me . . . The Hills Above

COLLECTED POEMS
  Twelve Years of Christmas
*A Man Alone
  With Love . . .
*The Carols of Christmas
  Seasons In The Sun
  Alone
  The Rod McKuen Omnibus

PROSE
*Finding My Father
*In His Own Words

COLLECTED LYRICS
*New Ballads
*Pastorale
*The Songs of Rod McKuen
*Grand Tour

*Not published in the United Kingdom

ROD McKUEN

The Sea Around Me . . .

The Hills Above

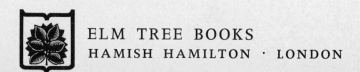

ELM TREE BOOKS
HAMISH HAMILTON · LONDON

First published in Great Britain, 1976
by Elm Tree Books Ltd
90 Great Russell Street, London WC1
Copyright © 1976 by Rod McKuen

The publication of this book in Great Britain marks its first appearance anywhere in the world.

Two of these poems are from *Listen To The Warm* © 1968 by Rod McKuen. Additional material in a different form was first published in *Sea Cycle, The Rod McKuen Folio, Seventeen* and the American edition of *Moment To Moment* © 1969, 1973, 1974, 1975, 1976 by Rod McKuen and Montcalm Productions. International copyright secured.

Further information may be obtained by contacting the Cheval/Stanyan Company, 8440 Santa Monica Boulevard, Los Angeles, Ca. 90069, USA, or the author's representative in Great Britain, Elm Tree Books Ltd.

ISBN 0 241 89505 7
ISBN 0 241 89538 3 (Limited edition)

Drawings and jacket design by Hy Fujita
Jacket photograph courtesy of KNBC, Los Angeles
Filmset by BAS Printers Limited, Wallop, Hampshire
Printed in Great Britain by
Lowe & Brydone Printers Ltd, Thetford, Norfolk

Tennyson was kicking up a great deal of earth by the roadside in the way he did when I stopped on a walk, pretending he had found a rabbit hole just beside me, but I barely took any notice of him, funny though he was.

Joan Fleming

This book is for an unnamed ocean,
that separates me from myself.

Contents

Author's Note

I have thought it true and for a long time lived by John Donne's ministry that 'no man is an island' and yet I do believe that for a while I have been just that—an island to myself. Separated, adrift—though not set apart, dreaming still that tanned Tarzan will swing down from some tree and rescue me or that a dozen sirens will come singing as they form a bridge from this place to the mainland (the mainland would be to be not *one*, but two).

I would not willingly be a sailor, leaving land too long a time. I could not live the life of some far fisherman, hip high in water every morning, dragging in the nets at night. But the ocean has always had a pull for me.

Something tugs and tugs, I've no doubt of that, something from the sea, whichever one I'm near. And when I stray too far from beachland I'm called back. What calls or carries me till I'm within the range of water once again is a mystery. I do know that the calm times, the quiet ones—not necessarily the best—have been lived out near the sea.

No man wants the hidden hand of anything to be his pilot. He should set out on some journeys with only maps of his own choosing; no compass but the one he carries in his head. Should he then sail beyond the earth's edge it will be his business only.

A year ago, I completed a book entitled *The Morning of My Life*. Shortly before its intended publication I withdrew it. The reasons, I suppose, are many. Most especially, on the printed page it came out more personal than I had expected. Without its publication there is a time lapse in my life.

The Morning of My Life is the first volume of an intended trilogy. This book is the second, to be followed by the final volume, *Sleep Warm*. So in your hands now, you have the middle. As my life has daily been revised, I've rewritten, rearranged it on the page.

The sea and the hills are this book's canvas. I have loved the hills— but they were always just above me, inaccessible. They seldom offered and never gave back love the way the ocean did.

That was before. There is a new ongoing miracle that has altered everything. And while I have the sea around me still, my new protector is the hills above—or perhaps I have mistaken tall towers in the town of London for protective hills.

ROD McKUEN
London, March, 1976/Los Angeles, April, 1976

The Sea Around Me

I

Buck had dreams
of giving Jimmy Dean
his rightful place
in the book of days.
He felt that I should help him
                    if I could.
I wanted only warmness
          and a chance to be
nobody else but me,
to live my life and my life only.

I think Buck finally understood.
One day he left the safety
                    of the beach
and travelled home
          to write his book.

Long letters used to come
from Iowa and Indiana
after Buck had left.
Come here he'd say,
there are corn-fed boys
          who bicycle
by the back porch
nearly every day,
interfering with my work
but adding to it.

Come here, come here
and help me make
          some apple-jack.

I still wanted warmness
not beneath an Indiana sun
but underneath the covers
                    anywhere.
I never went to Buck.
I answered
nearly every letter
with but a paragraph,
till the letters
     stopped arriving.

II

Lenny seized the winter
between his friendly teeth
and bit a chunk or two off
                  just for me.
I was left to wonder
more than ten years later
    if I stopped to thank him
              for the use
of his own heartbeat
          next to mine.

Lenny left for somewhere.
I'd get second-hand reports
*he's working in a restaurant
and now he's into water sports.*

No letter came from Lenny
in a dozen years.
I often thought of him
when I was wrapped
in woolly warmness
but more when I was not.

III

Aggie filled the beach bar
Sunday after Sunday
singing *Grandma Plays The Numbers*
her voice somewhere between a purr
and the steamboat's shout.

Aggie moved the men
who moved within the bar
then she moved herself
        back into town.

I saw a postcard once
she sent to someone else
        not me.
Honey, L.A.'s freaked
        and frigid
Your mother should have
gone to Bakersfield or Fresno.

Not Aggie, no.
In Bakersfield the jukebox
             kicks back shit
Grandma Plays The Numbers
                  wouldn't go.

I had Aggie's number
but not her line to call.
If I did I might have said
it's warm out here again
                  it is, it is
you should see me
I'm as brown as you.
Warmer than I was
             but not enough.

IV

Travellers on a summer Beach
in nineteen fifty-seven.
How could Santa Monica
have been so close to heaven?

One by one the houses
on the beachfront disappeared
the bay became a parking lot
Lenny's old apartment razed,
Buck's big house and loft
a new communal dwelling place.

I wish I had
the number and address
of all those friends
I knew and cared about
some twenty years ago
        in Santa Monica.

I'd like to write each one
                   and say
I'm warm, I am
for ever, always.
Someone has warmed me up
               who means it
and I won't be cold again.

I have no clues
and no addresses,
no leads on where
my old friends
          stop or play
and so I write to them
in books and journals
hoping they are reading
all the things
that I leave out.
          Not just
between the lines
but more ahead
and further back
          than that.

This book begins
as love leaves off
then goes with me
as I go on
from sea to sea
and back—alone.

Later
finally in the hills
love opens one more door.

As always
I expect this new experience
to be the lasting,
        final one.

As always
I come away
not beaten
or beat down
but less alive
and more confused.

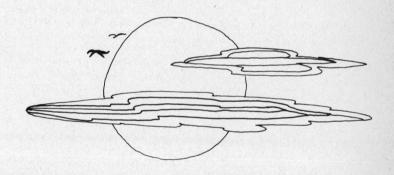

CALIFORNIA BEACHES

Starting Point

WITH A DUTCHMAN

With a Dutchman I went once
through Rembrandt Square
and down to Zandvoort, too.

I should have stayed
and lived my lifetime
    on that beach.

I might have been a sailor
singing songs to myself only
or to a friend in Amsterdam
who listened out of love.

I was always pulled by love
not only beds and bodies
but a city here,
        a red sail there.
A beach town
or some seaport city
always opened up her arms
in welcome to me.

I am now
the product of those
           many oceans
the sea is all I know
           for sure
but I know it well.

If the sea
did not make me
           by hand
it rubbed me, rolled me
out of darkness
           into light.
For I have seen
my past and future
on the white caps
dancing out beyond
a thousand shorelines.

I have recognized
            my face
swimming in the shallows,
my body blundering
through the grey-white foam.
My life has sailed
so far out past the tide
it's now beyond
my own far-reaching reach.

The sea makes *something*
out of *nothing* every day,
by the running in
and running back
of the tide alone.

And with the aid
of but a little sand
it polishes and hones
the bottom of the world
            twice daily.

One ocean for me
is not like any other
except to say
that each has given *comfort*
            when I needed it,
love when there was none
                  forthcoming
from another quarter,
peace if I stayed long enough
to wait for it or seek it out.

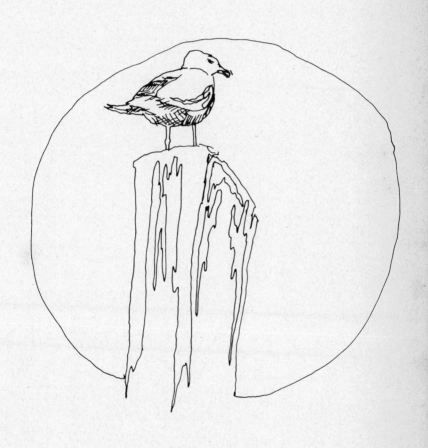

NETHERLANDS BEACH

Down the Dutch sea coast
to Blackberry on the low hills,
your skirts catching
on the underbrush
my boots trampling the grass.

Where are the sandstone cliffs
                and palisades?
Are they hiding somewhere
beneath blackberry vines
or were they never here
along these wide flat stretches,
aptly called The Netherlands.

The berries have embezzled
all the salt air
so that unlike other oceans
this air's sweet and thin.
I expect the berries
will be bitter.
The cost of this
last late October day.
Worth the price
                and more.

NEWPORT

Somewhere in Newport
there's a face I cupped
not out of love but out of need,
and that face wonders still
why I went away
after saying what I did.
Yet I'm so far beyond
the lies of Newport
I don't remember
what it was I said.

In North Beach, San Francisco
moving deliberately and slow
a love denied to me
walks home and not alone.

I couldn't find my way
through North Beach now
or down the long Pacific coast
with the aid of lies or love.

And I am not ashamed
though sometimes I go home afraid.

I worry only
that when love does come
I might not know its smile
                    for sure
or recognize its face.

So much is passed off,
praised and handed down
as love and loving
            in this life
that reality at best
must be unreal.

MORNING COLLECTION

In the half-light
we saw the swimmers
coming from the darkness
carrying the boy's body low,
as though its weight
was bending all of them
into the same submission.
As though the boy
was pulling them down now
the way the sea had pulled him
    to herself.

He was of course
just one more lover
of the grey-blue water.
A muscled boy who swam
a few yards farther out
               each day.
            But so young.
I wonder what he said
as he went down
that final time,
here I am or *let me go*?

I know the sea eats up
the men who love her most,
the way the killer queen
must finally one day
          reject the troops
who fought for her on battlefields
and fought with her in bedrooms.

I am not afraid.
I'd go down gladly in a whirlpool
if I had ridden all day
          on a friendly wave.

But one so young
colourless, not even gasping,
too dead for even lonely.
A conscience cannot even wonder
                    why.

For the sea
it was a little murder
done with might and yet no malice.
But what a poor repayment
for a man whose only crime
was to love the wild blue water
that in a single swallow
          tore and took him.

The sea gives up the living
as it does the recent dead,
at will it casts off what it will.

The ocean has a lesson
for our own lives
and those we take responsibility
                          towards.
Push forward it keeps saying
till your life is bare upon the shore
until you're naked to yourself
                          and God.
Yet the Christian and the Godless
are often washed together
and broken on the rocks.

To wade the water is to learn.

You'll gain a guideline,
a watermark just like the sea
that tells you how far you can travel
and still come home in certainty
                    and safety.

Morning people
tracking down the shore
retrieve the best
and see the very worst
the sea sheds on the beach.

*Hold on to me
and I'll become your enemy,
let me go and I'm your friend.*
The ocean says that every day
a thousand and a thousand times.
And every evening,
her words having pounded
in our heads all day,
we repeat them
to each other
            as our own.

So it is
that we confuse her speech
her language spoken
            wave to wave
and tide incoming
with those sentences
complex and simple
            we spit out
as dialogue invented.

The sea invents,
     we rearrange.
The sea takes out a patent,
          we infringe.
The sea holds copyright
to all the most important words,
speaking tongues that even time
          won't modify or use.

To those of us who've listened
the sea's the only teacher
teaching, and without a copybook.

Often she demands a bitter prize,
a head to batter on the rocks
a body to wash upon the shore
a smile to eat for breakfast
and though we wonder *why*,
it is the only question
that she leaves unanswered.

TREASURES

Seeking
more important treasures
than the common clam shell
every tide gives up,
I've been out collecting
bits of driftwood and debris
to decorate your dresser top.

A conch from where I shook
an irritated hermit crab,
other shells and stones
      of no importance
and a half-pint bottle,
amber in its colour
not yet chipped or broken.

Starfish, white
against the whiter sand
(I sailed the pink ones—
limp and living still)
back into the sea.
Some I'll find again
        tomorrow
midway through
      my morning walk.
Back they'll go
and back they'll come
another day, another hour later.

Some of us are only
treading water, hiking sand
             beach to beach
and not beyond,
pretending we're the sea's
                    extension
hoping we can pass it off.
Though we seldom do
we go on trying.

Riding out the rainstorms
             when we can.
Fighting off the fog
             with friendship,
sailing through each storm
with all the confidence
of those who reel in sails
nightly and for ever,
we tread the water
             like mosquitoes.

POPCORN

Making popcorn
for the seagulls on the porch
you look up from the stove
just long enough to look away.
Some new obscurity behind your eyes
I'm not as yet at liberty to know
stays lurking there
between the popcorn and the flame.

TRANSITION

Can you guess what's wrong?
I've tried and failed
to rise above the breakers
to swift sail out the storm.
Now the chance is going
         if not gone.
Will you be the one
to start the argument tonight
or is it my turn, I forget.

I wait here for a sign,
a motion wasted on me,
proof that it is possible
for each of us to care
    for each of us.

I cannot say
how long I've waited.
Years pass by within
a single hour
to those who feel uncared for.

Had there been a sign,
I would have known.

What goes on unseen
untold to us
        by one the other
is more real
than all the sentences
our senses spoke
                and speak.

I see your face and know
a tilting of your shoulder
speaks whole paragraphs aloud
whole stories filled with proof
that what is happening
is if anything a wilful lie
both of us indulge in.

This much is fact.
You do not amaze me
with your dark indifference.
You never once astound me
by being only what
        you wish to be.

I await the crumbs just now
delighted that they come
from fresh bread
        lifted out of ovens
by some hidden master baker.

No pride moves ahead
to pave my way.

I've fast become
the dark parts
        of your shadow,
little more than your extension,
hardly more than your left arm.

It tires me to know
I'm just the casing
        of a window
looking out beyond *your* world.

After I've packed up
                and gone
fly a flag
should the intruder come.

Take care to give me
fresh reports of all the ships
and all the ducks and seagulls
that sail or waddle beachward.

Be sure to tell me
if the seals come back
                this year
and how the house
gets through the winter.

Keep a diary of sorts
a notebook day to day
that I might thumb through
                or pore over
when I'm living inland
                        miles away.

THOUGHTS ON COURAGE

Had I the courage of one
I'd turn you around.
Had I the courage of five
I'd turn around inside you
pulling all the dark earth
                    with me.

Had I the courage of ten
we'd start so much together
that we'd never have the time
to finish one thing we'd begun.

Had I the courage of one hundred
I'd stand back and look at you,
then having filled my eyes
                    and lungs
I'd carry you so far away
that we'd reach seashores
              yet unseen
and bathe in water
even fish had not yet tested.

I am full and filled
with firm conviction
but courage comes in short supply.
Each of us can only work at it
              and try.

But gone you are
while still arriving.
Moving away, moving away.

Had I the courage of one
I'd run beside you
          or behind you.
Instead I turn the other way.

So it is we've started out
on this new day together
to travel parallel paths
in opposite directions.

NEGATIVE

I have carried several oceans
in my head for company
so that when I found myself
within the middle earth
I'd have water,
wide and deep enough
to wash the dirt
from every chamber
of my brain.

So assured was I
that I had water pictures
true and fixed for ever.
I came back down these dunes
towards the true sea
expecting nothing more
than what I'd thought up
                              yesterday.

But no one knows the ocean
unless they're sinking into it.
The shore is only shore
if you walk from it
to the ocean's edge and past
to be covered by its real
and not imagined wetness.
And so I cannot trust
my surest memory of you.

What did we have,
love at first
        and then some habit
an in-between, a purgatory need?
What made us come together?
        Can you say for sure?

Stay within the darkness
and from me
just a while longer
and you'll be
only one more pond
I thought to be an ocean.
Come to me
and our collective ocean
will wash over all our days
and troubles.

I don't believe that
but it's hard to let
so much loved
and unlived life
go without a speech.

A pity all things started
cannot finish at the summit.
Our lack of understanding
          one the other
leaves us by the roadside
as the giant wave goes by.

The holidays
are now beginning,
decorations everywhere.
What better time
to just let go?

I'll miss our language
and the lack of it
but I would rather
walk the empty
          midnight street
than share your Christmas frown.

They say
a comet's coming
through the sky
before the Twelfth Night
                    passes.
We needn't stay here
waiting for a signal
              or a sign.
What is finished
should be finally finished
not hung on to
              like a lifeline
that has finally stretched
              and snapped.

CHRISTMAS CARD

Where do they go
the people in our lives
that sail in like green leaves
and disappear like snow?
Not just in December
or the stormy winter months
but through the year and through the years.

Looking up a name today
I passed through three pages of G's
and found at least six names
I can't remember or never knew.

I addressed and sent
Christmas cards out and over to them
        all the same
for what if someone
            somewhere else
fingering his phone book
passed over those same names.
Happy Christmas G's and X, Y, Z's
and thank you for whatever care
or kindness you passed along to me
that my addled brain forgot.

You I remember
because of what you are
            to me.
Merry Christmas.

BIRDS

I

A band of birds,
geese I think,
flying in or back
from somewhere
to where the winter
will be less hard.

See them end to end
across the sky
hardly out of line
                by one.

Like a victory sign but wider
their formation is a marvel,
meticulous, mechanical.

And there
just above those trees
another band of birds
brings up the rear,
like a vanguard
keeping guard.

Some have landed,
and they rest
on bare-limbed trees
and telephone lines.
They dot but never blur
the moon.

Perched still and silent
awaiting their rotation,
strung out they spy
in Morse code.

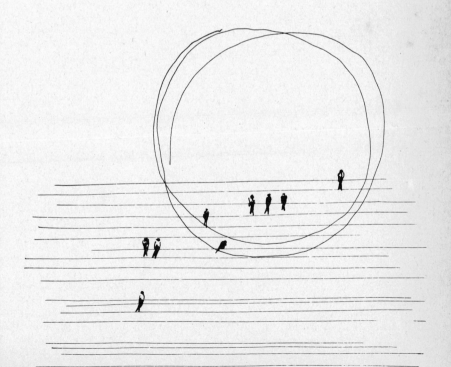

II

Rested, restless now
they move as one.
Picking up formation
they fly straight forward
                overhead
blinking in the sunlight
till a better place to perch
                is found.

I stumbled on your suitcase
            in the hallway
half an hour ago.
Have you been looking
out the window
            at the birds?

I have seen you move so often.
Set sail on so much
            unknown sea
that I can feel the readiness
within you to be gone
but this time
I'll do all the running.
You needn't fly or migrate
            with the birds.

Stay.
I wish you life
in great abundance
down your lifetime.
Whoever's coming,
known or unknown
on his way to you
I pray that he
will not be long
in finding you.

Don't forget
to send a postcard
telling me the news.
Did the seals
come back this year,
did the grunion run
and did you out-distance
all the near and distant strangers,
capture them and captivate them
                    one by one?

Write me.
I'd be unhappy if I thought
that you were still out running
and had not been caught.

Tomorrow
I'll be that lone bird
winging past the morning moon
on my way below
the belt of California.

MEXICO

A House By The Sea

FRIDAY WALK

This morning's walk produced no shells of any great variety, though the beach was up and about its daily business, early and on time. Sand dollars, finding themselves naked on the shore slid into sand like flying saucers burrowing in the earth, caught in an alien country and forced to hide. Sand crabs still drill deep to set up housekeeping. A great, uncommon bloated fish washed up on the shore some days before, grows fatter now in the sea air and the sun.

I am not looking, only open for the finding, and to be found out finally.

BEACH DIARY

I

The sun full measured
this second day
of this fourth year
of coming back
    and coming back
and coming back again
        to Mexico.

In the trees it crouches now
       until it springs out
harsher than remembered
to bake me through the noon.

Siestas notwithstanding
the heat has got them all
impatient, amorous
       or ambitious.

Lizards in the patio
squaring off at either end
then racing down the tile
towards each other,
hind ends reared
and hind legs stiffened,
they snap and scatter
in the dance of courtship.

In the end
        like movie dinosaurs
they clash and roll
in twisted knots
the balance of the afternoon.

Having seen the ritual
acted out and realized
I started back to sleep
beneath the kindest sky
I've known in twenty months.

Suddenly they're in the hedge.
Rustling, threading through
                the roots.
Tunnelling
in the dead-leaf carpeting.
                Whoosh,
and one comes flying
through the thicket
like an alligator given wings.

At midday
a school of dolphins
surface sink and zig-zag by
heading northward in the noon
then back again at sunset.

Too far out to swim to
but close enough to see
arching up and down
            amid the waves
like tumblers in a circus,
who hit the net
then bounce into the air
            and somersault again.

Later
when the sun
starts slumping seaward
it will be the gulls' turn
to file through the air
in bad formation.

Not as agile as the sparrows
nor as graceful as wild geese
jetting home at spring,
these troop transport gulls
                    are clumsy.

Fuel tanks full
you can almost see
their sleep beginning
as they fly, no, stumble by.

Sand crabs again
           scrambling sideways
dragging battered burdens
through the soft red sunset.
A fish head gorged up by a gull
twice the sand crab's size.
Another darts off easily
with half a clam.

My long shadow passing past them
is enough to send each recluse
down his well-dug hole.

Could I invade this spider diary
I might turn up
the seashore chronicle
of one whole winter
or a pattern more elaborate
than the tank-like tracks
of a thousand sand crabs
invading that first atoll
past and all along
           the shoreline.

Evening
and a single gecko's
loud percussion
heard above the waves
        above the wind
above the crickets,
not yet chorusing
but making ready.

Geckos everywhere.
Between the roof beams
along the stuccoed wall
above the arch
of every doorway.

A dozen now. More.
Pale off-white in colour
            almost yellow.
Only slightly darker
than the once-white plaster.

Hanging on,
upside down and sideways.
Not moving, not sleeping.
Geckos. Not like crystal.
Not hard like alabaster.
More like marzipan.
Fragile looking.

The gecko's
vocal clattering
somewhere beyond
              the shutters
never seems
to get an answer.
              He clicks
at all the unexpected times
like castanets gone crazy
and without a master.

He's been here since
                the pinto morning.
Little runs he makes
then stopping to survey
a bee or fly
his long tongue
takes them by surprise
quicker and more sure
than any angler.
                Agile as an angel.

The gecko sounds again.
The echo through the arches
                could be one or five.
Tambourines in double time.

I half expect
that Spanish dancers
will come bursting through the door,
vests and petticoats of every colour
heels stomping, snapping, clicking
ready for some fine fiesta.

The day
has opened up,
progressed and gone.
I've watched it move
from the lizard's lost siesta
to Don Quixote of La Mancha's
imagined but not held
                        fiesta.

Stars.
A few are falling.
No comet yet,
but it's expected.

II

With the stars
all stringing out and strung
and the moon half hung
            and hanging,
hunger starts somewhere
within my belly.
It will not be gone
with bowls of guacamole,
            as it didn't go
with friends and family
commiserating on my loss.

I elected
to come down
to this house
and to this beach
knowing that I couldn't
leave all memory,
            fact or fiction
in an overcoat at home.

Soon the crickets
will stop adding,
counting, summing up.

The heavy air will set all things
            to sleeping
and the steady rhythm
of this well-loved,
            well-known ocean
will conspire to keep us there.

That battle won,
another day makes ready
            to arrive,
another night to follow.

More defeats
or maybe victories
            wait ahead.
I will have to meet
and battle each alone,
but the victory party
isn't worth the having
if the celebration's done
            in solitary.

III

Was there rehearsal,
a time of trying out
how many starts
            and stops occurred
before the balls
fell into place?

Awhile back, I know,
but how far back
            and when?
These questions done
        and finally answered
I hope they'll not
        be asked again.

This is the way it was
while I was waiting for your eyes
                    to find me.

I was drifting
          going no place.
Hypnotized by sunshine
                    maybe,
barking back at seals along the beach.
Skipping flat stones on the water,
but much too wise for sand castles.
My castles were across the sea
or still within my mind.

There were the beach bars
and the other brown beach people
sometimes little bedrooms
                    were my beach,
but I was drifting, going no place.

I must have thought
the night could save me
as I went down into pillows
looked up through dirty windows
smiled back from broken mattresses
turned in Thunderbirds
*   and kissed in elevators.*

I cried too sometimes.
*   For me.*

I loved every face
I thought looked pretty
and every kindred eye
I caught in crowds.
But I was drifting
*   before you.*

Who I said it for
should not be paramount
              or prime
only that I wrote
and said it once.
              Got it out
and out from under me,
delivered it in time
to start the chain,
broken often,
but always mended.

Too much sun
within those endless summers
has made my mind forget
whose pleasure prisoner I was
when the knot was tied.
Who I pretended to
or who pretended to me
that we were living out
the lovers' dream.

The most important thing I am
is a guardian of dreams,
the least important
          thing I am
            is me.

Hurry someone.
Another week and I'll be ready.

FISHERMAN

I

Brown fishermen
have reaped their harvest
one more day
   and now head slowly home,
half a truckload of them.

Legs dangling
from the back end of a pickup
their eyes not leaving
that long white line
that crawls out evenly below.

The cough
and sputter truck
hugs the shoulder
of the mountain road
climbing slower
as the hill gets higher.

Faster cars wait, honk
grumble back behind it
in a head to tail-light line.
Then chancing
            on the widest curve
sail by at racetrack speed.

Still mute and mesmerized
by tiredness
        and that white stripe
brown fishermen head home.

II

The birds went looking
· all the afternoon
for what whitebait
the fishermen had left
                    behind.
I glanced up too
half expecting some brown body
to come slowly down the sand.
What better way to waste my time
than in dreams of glory?

Many did
and many do
come down the beach.
Running, strutting,
                    sauntering,
diving in the water
sliding in the sand.
Surely one will stop
            or look.

Take your time
brown-bodied strangers
I've more hours
than there are stones
along the coastline.

Impatience has been
            till now
an overriding trouble
        in my life
but I'll not be
        impatient any more.
The sun has calmed me,
charmed me into waiting.
I pace myself
the way the sea birds do.

I do not expect
the boys of boredom
to come barging, bolting
            down the sand.
I would rather they moved
                    slowly
so that I can search them out.

I'd not wish to see
the girls of summer
parading past me
            in a pageant.
Let them file by single file
giving this one man
the chance to twice them over
not look one time, then away.

Surely
as this summer starts
there is mermaid, merman
                somewhere
who will walk or wander by
causing me to have a cause,
a purpose for the year
                        upcoming.

If not I have
the mother ocean still
but making love to relatives
                is not as full
and all fulfilling
as being filled by strangers
                or filling up
a proper stranger's arms.

IDLE UNDER SUN

Once I thought
ideas were exceptions
            not the rule.
That is not so
they are so plentiful
that they ride by
                on air.
You've only to reach out
and snatch one
from the mist
or from nowhere.

With little raw material but sand
                the sea has made
two hundred thousand mountains
that we'll likely never know.

This being so
is it too much to ask
that each man in his lifetime
makes a single contribution,
both unique and useful,
that no man walking down the beach
has handed us before?

Why not pay back
            our birth bill
by adding an idea
            even two or six
to the many given us
without condition
            or a price?

MONDAY BEACH

My life
is bought and paid for.
It does not belong to God
or any man now drawing breath.
I am free to give it as a whole
to any ocean of my liking
or dismantle it in private
              piece by piece
by pills or poetry,
the poison of just letting go
or any other means
        I think befitting
    of the public hero
           and the private coward.

Stop me I say to me;
stay my hand
should it be steady
        in its new resolve.
And yet I do believe
that like the tide
my life has come
                and gone
in circle after circle.

I've been dead
and resurrected
        many times.
Who's to say
it cannot happen yet again?

POSTCARD HOME

The first sail of the day
           and it comes closer.

This morning
when I took my sea walk
small fish were flopped up
all along the shore.
Gills muddy and still gasping,
too many to throw back.

Mexican children,
four or five ahead of me
ran and laughed
and popped fresh fish
into woven baskets
then went away
their baskets full
           and overflowing,
laughing still and happy.

The children's noisy shrieks
are gone but stay here still
mixed with a wind just coming up
and set the sand to skipping rope
                    and dancing.

Tell those at home hello
and that I'm coming back
even if it's just to stop awhile
before I go away again.

It's raining
on the airport road
so I'll not start today,
            perhaps tomorrow,
but I'll be coming back
            before the week is out.

THE FIRST

No matter when I start
that first day's walk
along the tide's white ragged edge,
someone's been ahead of me.

I went at noon the first day,
            ten the next.
Finally at sunrise
I started out each day.
And on this very morning
I was up before the sun
guided by the whitecaps only
luminous in the dimming starlight.

When at last the light
began to rim the far horizon
I saw beside my own, new footprints
in the Monday sand
a larger imprint trailing on
                ahead of me.
And beside that widened stride
        on this quiet beach
the soft impression of a dog
who must have trotted
by his master's side.

I've but one more morning
left to me
before I trade Tres Vidas
　　　　　for the city,
but if I have to start out
down the beach at midnight
　　　　　　　or before
I'm determined to confront
that brown beach man
who dares to think
he loves my ocean
more than I do.

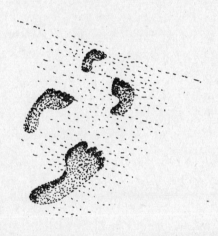

THE END OF JANUARY

The ocean rumbles on. Wave after wave, one over the other, faster than the preceding wave recedes. On the far horizon, nothing. As far as I can see at either end, nothing.

A small rain came this morning. No trace of it now, not on shore or sea. A school—or at most, half a dozen sharks zigzagged back and forth when the sea was calmer. Earlier a man walked down the beach. Never bending. Not stopping. Not collecting.

Far into January we are. Almost at the end. The comet didn't come. I watched some nights, got up early several mornings, but if a comet came or went or stays above me I failed to pick it out from all the other stars. Stars there are at night, aplenty.

If I knew why I had the need to travel out of my own room, my space, to anywhere, I might be able to explain what's gone or isn't coming.

As this out-of-season summer rolls beneath me and away, I wait. The mystery of the sea's no clearer than it was for me before. Worse, the mystery of myself grows harder to discern.

I've had my fist inside the world and felt for sure I was its axis. I've seen the kings go by, though I'll admit my vantage point was from some distance. For derring-do I've sailed through clouds more easily than I once floated on a pond. However jerry-built my life has been, I've felt there was solidity of sorts. In truth there is, however little. I built what I thought needed building—some would say security, I'd still say solidity for some *one*.

There must have been a blueprint once. Now, no trace of any master plan remains. As nobody stops or stays here still.

I do not brood. I am not malcontent. I am not. Where once I had opinions good and bad of what I'd done, even to myself, I have none now.

It, whatever that should be or is, is out there surely. I can't believe it never started, never was. I still have this life, half built—unfinished, waiting to be taken by, given to, some *one*. It was never made exclusively for me. There are takers, just that, but none that I would willingly turn my living over to. Still that's the one desire I have that overrides all others, to give, to let go of whatever I have learned, collected or amassed.

I wonder how long I can move, go through the motions, knowing what I know. How many years or days are left? Why go through the motions anyway?
I don't know.

I am waiting. I will do so, while I can.

The Hills Above

HILLS AND LOWER HILLS

I sit at times as quiet as an unwound clock and hear my own heart pounding, beating, tearing up the inside of my chest. It's then that I need noise. The radio, the gramophone, the downtown street, the dogs that outside bark in harmony then unison just to break the silence.

Sometimes I do despair of love but then again it's all there, must be up ahead or anywhere. Why else would we go on, why would we continue to move forward or stand still?

I do wonder at the signposts and the neon signs announcing coming miracles. They are as sure as silver and as true as truth can be.

When I look back now I am positive the warning bell went off and yet I stumbled forward, unprepared for magic, ill prepared for you.

Hills have happened in my life. Hills and lower hills. Today I see no low hills. Everything ahead looks high and getting higher.

Too much comes and goes beneath the surface of the sea for any mind to comprehend. Will this be true as I hike hills and higher hills?

At times I feel I know the sea. At least I'm well aware of its consistency while in the midst of change. Will it take me long to know a mountainside; consider it as a familiar? Is there mystery within the mountains and do the shadows coming down at twilight make only changes on the surface or is there a depth within the hills themselves, as within a wave?

Since I seek solitude and safety from the hills now, the same or near the same as I've received from ocean after ocean, I need answers sure and true. And soon.

MEETING

I admit that I am shy.
More so with those faces
and those forms
that I start to love
with but one look only.

Back in the room
we had no liquor
        and no radio
no aphrodisiac but need.
Oh, I needed you. I did, I do.

Your bushy head and your big eyes,
your thighs to wrap myself around,
your intermittent smile and stare.
Your caring for me then and now.

I pushed a pillow
soft beneath your head
and murmured love
from the beginning.

I knew. Don't ask me how.
That we were starting
what could not be finished
                in our lifetimes.

Here we are
and those tomorrows
left or owed to me,
borrowed and as yet
            unbought for you
will not be enough.
We should move
towards the heavens
or at least above the earth
                somewhere
                for always.

Though I know
need is not enough
        perhaps this time
simple wanting
will transcend all this
        and everything.

MIDDLE NIGHT CONFUSION

As the sun has just now
bent down into the ocean,
bend down to me.
Rising up
I promise you'll not frown.

As the stars
begin appearing
move in closer
begin to pull me
                    to you
as I pull you down.

As we roll sideways
see the path of moonlight
stretching on the water
wide enough to walk on
with an army
if one of us was God.

God is here somewhere
                    between us.
I can touch and feel Him
lying up against
                    your back,
one arm extended
through the roof
exchanging bulbs
in burnt-out stars.

But wait
there is no beach at all.
No moonlight on the water
no waves sing out to me.
Can this be so,
that in these hills
away from everything
        I knew before,
the only singing
            my ears hear
is your sighs,
heavy full of thunder?

One more time
and one more time again.
You are my ocean
        and my stars,
my God and all his heaven.
And life for me begins.

Beach-bar lingo
being all the same
we were left to make
whole conversations
             with our eyes.

Add to this
that glances must be tentative
for none should know our business
                  but ourselves.

I wonder then
that we met at all.
Perhaps the language
        of the desperate
is the strongest one yet made.

How else could you explain
an understanding without words?
A moving out the door
with no pre-arrangement?

PRISON

Leaning up against the wall
           in the half-light
I couldn't let you pass
without one final smile.

So it was
I tiredly undressed again
and ate your eyes
and your eyes only
    for breakfast.

You were dressed
as I undressed
three steps took you
        to the door.

I cannot stay
within this room alone
or crawl back into bed
without your being here.

I am a prisoner
in my own gaol,
for what place can I go
if I can't follow,
            be with you?

My brain and stomach
both are empty.
My insides drain
as each hour passes
outside your eyes
            and company.

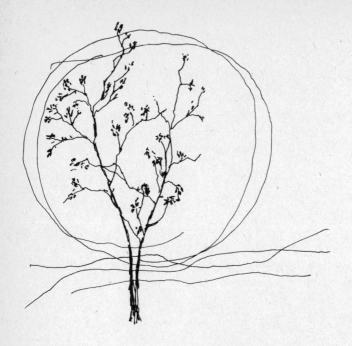

The only thing I know
is your full body
all else has been
erased for me.

REDWOOD CITY POEM

You asked me
what the word
before good-bye is,
I replied Hello
and it was so.

You were pulling from me
even as we met
even as we touched
        the earth
making ready to move skyward
you were heading back
        into the trees.

What kind of world
have I made
    for myself
that drives you from me
apologizing as you go?

If you had been the first
that went away unsmiling
I might have questioned you
or mumbled as to mood
        and motive
but there's a pattern here
unfolding like the same scenario
every time I open up.
           Every time.

Beyond hello, before good-bye
           there should be
a string of words
or one long paragraph
to make the ending easy.

With so little time together
how could you determine
           or even guess
it wouldn't work,
get better or move upward?
Does youth give you
           special knowledge?

That I did not meet
your expectations
makes me sorry
but I am not surprised.
Still, why did you allow me,
give me dispensation,
to involve you in my life?

BOXER

I am so amazed
at finding out
my head still reels
under even friendly blows
that I'm determined
not to let the boxer
        or the battler
come in close again.

I will not willingly go out
into the evening any more
and place myself within
that enchanted circle,
the moving staircase
        or the rain.

I should stay at home
behind the iron gates
        and rainbow glass.
Sure places I've constructed.
The disappointments yet to come
can be lived by me in private.
No one need know
if the wounds are fatal
or if I'm waiting out
            some healing time.

There is an emptiness
and it is deep.
A wound so old
that healing wouldn't work.

If I have not yet
come back around
to where I started
then I am only inches
from that now narrow
                    corridor
meant to bring me there.

I AM HEADING HOMEWARD

Arms full of promises
beds full of dreams
a head full of songs and none—
no one to hear them
at close quarters.

I am heading homeward
homeward bound am I
        travelling from
the farthest point north
        in California
to its middle and to home.

Having felt your strength
come into me
from the first long touch
to the last hand clasp
I am stronger now.

But I am weak for wanting,
tied up in knots from so much need,
wound in a ball and doubled over
from happenstance
that wouldn't, will not
        go on happening.

Stopped still am I
from your so fragile so firm hand.
You left me more a boy
              and less a man
than I might have cared to be.

Listen to me
I am finally going home
to double over and be sick
on my own ground
to weep my guts out
in my own back yard.

Leaving you was hard.
Your leaving harder.
I am going home to bear witness
to your having been with me
and some time up ahead
if I am living and still looking
I'll restock the larder
now pulled down
with a slow deliberate pull.

I am still together
heading home
              but not sure how.

Though we'll not meet again
I'll still be melding into you
                    and sweating,
standing next to you, unsteady,
facing you afraid for always.
Down the never-ending
                    middle nights
out and over all the days
that may be left to me.

Your leaving gave me
my own birthmark
like the clot inside
            some feeble
and unbalanced head.
I wear it up above my heart
my own red badge of courage,
my own and only birthmark
        attesting to my birth
                whenever.

I heading homeward
    let me go.
The heart grows tired,
timid and afraid sometimes.
It needs to rest
as much as any head
on aching shoulders.

If I can go on
dreaming up safe seas
            and seaweed
my mind will still stay well,
but this old heart
grown older by its own mistakes
needs resting and a resting place.

SUNDAY EVENING

I

I could see
Mount Shasta when you called,
the snow and everything.
The trees and all the wrong roads
I took getting out of town.

I could feel the chill air
we'd gone walking in
    two nights past
and both your arms about me
        later in the room.

I could see your eyes
            so well
that I was half afraid
if I reached out
        ahead of me
I might have touched them,
                worse
that I might not.

You were back inside my life
explaining how you hadn't gone.
We were speeding, racing
                far ahead
beyond and into years
        that hadn't come.

Here it was
the happy ending coming up.
        The summing up.

The letters start now.
Absence face to face
necessitates the printed word.

Your first letter
        came today.
So much love leapt word to word
that I reread each paragraph
sure that I had done the writing
sent the missive off to you.

Your letter came
some scribblings on paper
a document to rank
with all the freedom treaties
        yet thought up.

II

More letters on the unlined page.
A month and we'll be home
                    together,
three weeks even less.
I love you, said on postcards
to titillate the mailman,
my crotch and head and mind
            alike and all at once.

Give me your hand across the ocean
hold it out and I'll be there.

I die, no—I am living well
basking in your now imagined smile,
praising polaroid for pictures
showing me your blue-red grin
bringing you each night to me
   home again, home again.

When I went away
I never changed my watch.
Believe that or believe it not.
Whatever time the true time was
it was only time.

I remained convinced
   and still believing
though we stood apart
that I was part of you.

MIDDLE CALIFORNIA

And Beyond

ALTERNATIVES

I have heard there are alternatives. To what, I say. To living, a man can always die. Ah, but that's the hard way out. The easy way is to go on living. I have so much life and living that needs doing I'm surprised I ever thought of death. You've but to smile at me in morning and a new life starts. When you frown that will be my excuse to live a while longer in order that I might coax a new smile out of you.

The only alternative is to be without you. I cannot imagine that now and so no alternatives exist for me. That does not mean I'm unafraid. I would that I had left to me one safety-zone. One place that I might come to, one island I might row to should you run from me.

MIDNIGHT SAVIOUR

Have you come
   to save me?
      Very well.

I'm teetering
between the earth
     and hell.
I'll gladly take salvation
over pot and pills
   and cheap red wine.
I'm grateful for your arms
but open up a little more
so that I need not love you
     out of gratitude
but only for yourself.
Let me lie against your belly
inhaling all the night air
    you let out.

Let me reach inside you
slow and easy, deliberate
so that your anatomy
will be my primer,
your sighs now heavy
my own northwest wind.
            Let me probe
a secret place
no one else
            has so far touched.

Allow me this small favour
to pull you to me from the inside,
to live inside you half of every night.
            The star-filled half.

Don't be discouraged
if I fumble or become inept.
I'll try again,
            now slower still.

Then moving to your face
your eyes will dazzle me
as our mouths match,
the insides probing
one another's insides.

Slide next to me. See,
no position is uncomfortable
            or wrong.

Such space there is between your back
and each new morning.
Such emptiness
my body and the sunlight
            cannot fill.
I'll try, I will.

Remember that you caught me
on the heels of what I thought
            was love.

SUNSET COLOURS

I love the sunset colours
    not just in spring
but every day
that God is good enough
to share his red and orange
             and yellow
with me
    and mine.

Lately I sleep late
and so I seldom see
      the scarlet morning
or the gold behind the trees.

I depend a lot on sunsets.
Even when no sunset comes
I fill my head
with all the sunshine past
and sunsets that I know will come.

Looking in your eyes
I see the sun come
even in the darkness.

Do you know how much
              I feel for you
and in what kind of way?
              I feel the world for you
and in every way.
I think sometimes
              that I'll explode,
        die or disappear
before I have the chance
to say to you
just how I feel.

Don't let it be today.

FLYING FREE

I believe that flying free
is letting go.
That all above the sun
and in the sunshine
    waits for me
because I want to know.

I believe that flying free
is staying unattached
       to anything.
Not tied down by the sky
or the tended tether line.

I believe that I'll fly free
only if I do not go
    by myself, alone.
That I'll stay chained
unless I'm soaring side by side
     or inside someone.
I believe in you
and that's the same as flying free.

I contradict myself
because I am attached to you.
But still I'm flying free.

MIND MINDER

A butterfly flies up
inside my head,
consuming all my early years
the memory of just yesterday,
other loves and lives
I might have known or knew.

He sits and eats away
within that place I've lived
where he now lives.

Please remember for me
all those things
that need remembering.
Let me use your head
            as mine.

I ask that you
attempt to lead me,
to carry me aloft
bend down to scoop me up,
to ferry me across my life
as you would a child
across a too deep river.
You are the end of me,
and my new beginning.

You are my brother
          and my wife.
My lover and my son.
My mother and my husband
          my teacher
and the one I long to teach.

The woman
that I dreamed of finding
the friend who never was.

You transcend gender,
eliminate September,
add another month of Sundays
to a calendar well worn.

I will be for you
                whatever works.
I will work to make you *be*,
while you eliminate
the buzzing, ringing sound
that permeates my brain
                of late.

A butterfly
and maybe more
is buzzing in my head.
If he should eat it all away
you've head enough for both of us.

If caterpillars crawl
down through my brain
you've brain enough
to see us both through
this thing that has seized me,
seized us both at once.

IN CASE YOU DIDN'T KNOW

Some days up ahead
will come down empty
and some years fuller
than the fullest one
we've known before.

Today has been
the best day yet.

        I thought
you ought to know that,
and I thought it time
that I said *thank you*
for whatever might have
passed between us
that in your mind
you might have felt
missed my attention.

It didn't
and it doesn't
and it won't.

Thank you
for the everydays
that you make
        into holidays.

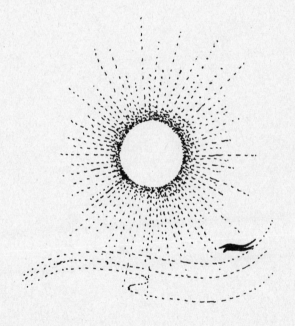

ADDENDUM

Time Step

AU SUIVANT

Time does its dance again. Out of focus, out of frame. Clicking in and out time zeros all these years the bedside clock, or that one that ticks inside me, has now become confused.

The circle now completes itself. I regret nothing. I expect the *next* experience will be the lasting final one.

TIME ENOUGH

Find me friendly beasts
and I'll lie down
between their legs
easy and with ease.

Show me quiet shores
and I'll run down them
endlessly and without end
till my feet have blisters
from the polished sand.

Give me time enough
and I'll unwind, unset
all the clocks and watches
in the worldly world
so that I'll have time enough
to hike down quiet shores
with friendly beasts.

Should they seek me out
I'll go forward eagerly
with the wildest of the animals.

That friendliest of all the animals
that paces from the bedside now
      moving with no little grace
and understanding
does so out of knowledge
            and some love.

I fear, no, I am sure
the kindness I've discerned as love
            is limited.

A pity
for even as I feel
the end approaching
I still hold nothing back.
I am guilty only
of some dark suspicions.

I know now space and time are coming.
Enough to give me every hour
the new-maths needs
for adding, multiplying and dividing
emptiness and dust and ceiling cracks.

Those friends I knew in Santa Monica
all those many years ago
had in common
              a sense of time.
Time and timing's everything.

I waited just a minute longer than I should.
Alas, a single minute lost
                  is not made up.

Again, I lie here in a quandary.
Which way now?
Back towards the sea?
Hike a higher hill? Where?

Some new cracks have appeared
            across the ceiling.
They were not there
last week or yesterday
and no new earthquake
rattled at the window
or was reported on the radio.

Have I been so busy
trying to live out
        this latest dream
that wreckers came
while I was fast asleep
to tear away the final cover?

My head is turning slowly
now unhurried like this April day.
I expect that in the year
            yet coming
I will somewhere, if not here,
        once again sleep warm.

About the author . . . . . .

Rod McKuen's books of poetry have sold in excess of sixteen million copies in hardcover, making him the bestselling and most widely read poet of our times. In addition he is the best-selling living author writing in any hardcover medium today. His poetry is taught and studied in schools, colleges, universities and seminaries throughout the world.

Mr McKuen is the composer of more than fifteen hundred songs that have been translated into Spanish, French, Dutch, German, Russian, Japanese, Czechoslovakian, Chinese, Norwegian, Afrikaans and Italian, among other languages. They account for the sale of more than one hundred eighty million records. His songs include: 'Jean', 'Love's Been Good To Me', 'The Importance of the Rose', 'Ally Ally, Oxen Free', and several dozen songs with French composer Jacques Brel, including: 'If You Go Away', 'Come Jef', 'Port of Amsterdam', and 'Seasons in the Sun'. Both writers term their writing habits together as three distinct methods; collaboration, adaptation and translation.

Mr McKuen's film music has twice been nominated for Motion Picture Academy Awards (*The Prime of Miss Jean Brodie* and *A Boy Named Charlie Brown*). His classical music, including symphonies, concertos, piano sonatas and his very popular *Adagio for Harp and Strings,* is performed by leading orchestras. In May 1972, the Royal Philharmonic Orchestra in London premiered his *Concerto No. 3 for Piano & Orchestra,* and a suite, *The Plains of My Country.* In 1973, the Louisville Orchestra commissioned Mr McKuen to compose a Suite for Orchestra and Narrator, entitled *The City.* It was premiered in Louisville and Danville, Kentucky in October, 1973, and was subsequently nominated for a Pulitzer Prize in Music. He has been given a new commission by the City of Portsmouth for a symphonic work to commemorate that City's friendship with Australia. The new work will be premiered in 1977, both in Portsmouth and Australia's new Sydney Opera House.

His *Symphony No. 3,* commissioned by the Menninger Foundation in honour of their fiftieth anniversary, was premiered in 1975 in Topeka, Kansas.

Before becoming a best-selling author and composer, Mr McKuen worked as a labourer, radio disc jockey and newspaper columnist, among a dozen other occupations. He spent two years in the Army, during and after the Korean War.

Rod McKuen makes his home in California in a rambling Spanish house, which he shares with a menagerie of old English sheep dogs and a dozen cats. He likes outdoor sports and driving and has recently taken up flying.

As a balloonist he has flown in the skies above the western United States and recently in South Africa. He is the subject of a new feature-length film on ballooning entitled *Rod McKuen: Flying Free.*

The author has recently completed the libretto and music for a new opera, *The Black Eagle*, and his first book of prose, *Finding My Father,* has just been published by Coward-McCann in America. *The Sea Around Me . . . The Hills Above* is his first book for Elm Tree Books/Hamish Hamilton and his first work to have initial publication in Great Britain.

Much of the author's time is now spent working for and with his non-profit foundation, Animal Concern. He is at present completing a second volume of prose.